PAUL
KARIYA

PAUL KARIYA

HOCKEY MAGICIAN

Jeff Savage

Lerner Publications Company • Minneapolis

For Patrick Thomas Conroy—my nephew magician

This book is available in two editions:
Library binding by Lerner Publications Company
Soft cover by First Avenue Editions
241 First Avenue North, Minneapolis, MN 55401

Website address: www.lernerbooks.com

Library of Congress Cataloging-in-Publication Data

Savage, Jeff, 1961–
    Paul Kariya, hockey magician / Jeff Savage.
        p.   cm.
    Includes bibliographical references and index.
    Summary: A biography of this young Japanese-Canadian hockey player who plays for the Mighty Ducks of Anaheim.
    ISBN 0–8225–3661–7 (lib. bdg. : alk. paper). —
ISBN 0–8225–9824–8 (pbk. : alk. paper)
    1. Kariya, Paul, 1974–   —Juvenile literature. 2. Hockey players—Canada—Biography—Juvenile literature. [1. Kariya, Paul, 1974–   . 2. Hockey players. 3. Mighty Ducks of Anaheim (Hockey team) 4. Japanese—Canada—Biography.] I. Title.
GV848.5.K37S28   1998
796.962'092 — dc21
    [B]   97–41050

Manufactured in the United States of America
1 2 3 4 5 6 – JR – 04 03 02 01 00 99

Contents

1

Picture Perfect

Paul Kariya (ka-REE-yuh) glanced at the clock on the wall. It was six thirty. One hour until game time. He chewed the last few bites of his spaghetti and vegetables and got up from the training table. It was time to put on his uniform. He went into the locker room to get dressed.

Paul tried to pretend this was just another game. He smiled to his teammates as he walked to his locker. Amidst the chatter in the room, Paul sat down and quietly began putting on his protective gear. Knee pads, shin guards, elbow pads, shoulder guards—hockey players wear a lot of gear, so it took Paul some time to get dressed. As he did so, he thought about the game. He couldn't help feeling a bit nervous. Paul's team, the Anaheim Mighty Ducks, was in the National Hockey League playoffs for the first time.

The Mighty Ducks were about to play the Phoenix Coyotes in Game 1 of the 1997 Western Conference quarterfinals series. Although Paul was just 22 years old, he had already played in nearly 200 games for the Mighty Ducks. He was the team's all-time leader in goals, assists, points, shots, **power-play** goals, **shorthanded** goals, game-winning goals, overtime goals, and just about everything else. But as good as he was, he had never played in a game as big as this.

As Paul bent forward to lace up his skates, he imagined being out on the ice. He pictured himself skating along the boards and stealing the puck. He imagined making a perfect pass to a teammate. He imagined getting the puck back and firing a **wrist shot** for a goal. When he finished tying his skates, Paul remained hunched over, still visualizing the game. "I think the mind is the most important part of all sports," Paul has said. He pictures himself playing like this before every game. His teammates know to leave him alone.

At last Paul stood to finish getting dressed. He pulled his jersey over his head. It was white, trimmed in jade, purple, and silver, with the familiar duck head-shaped hockey mask on the front. The number 9 appeared on both sides with the letters K-A-R-I-Y-A stitched across the back. The great Wayne Gretzky's number 99 jersey had long been the most popular-selling jersey in North America, but for nearly a year now, Paul's number 9 Ducks jersey had been the fans' favorite. Paul tucked the corner of his jersey into his pants, just like his idol Gretzky, and left with his teammates out the door.

As he walked down the tunnel to the rink, the uproar reminded Paul that this would be no ordinary game.

Wild Wing, the Mighty Ducks' mascot, rouses the crowd inside Arrowhead Pond—Anaheim's hockey stadium.

The Arrowhead Pond of Anaheim was always sold out, and the 17,174 fans always made plenty of noise, but this time Paul could hear something special, something more. When he emerged from the tunnel with his teammates he saw a sea of white in the stands. In celebration of their team making the National Hockey League playoffs, the Mighty Duck fans had dressed in white. What's more, they were twirling and swirling white towels. The Ducks skated onto the ice to a burst of cheers and whistles.

The Mighty Ducks line up for the national anthem.

As Paul lined up with his teammates for the national anthem, he stood out as the smallest player on his team. At 5 feet 11 inches and 175 pounds, he only comes up to most other players' shoulders. He is handsome, with jet black hair and olive skin, and his boyish smile rivals that of Mickey Mouse. The Disney Corporation owns the Mighty Ducks, making the team a perfect fit for Paul, who is as popular as a Disney character himself.

The starters took the ice. Paul, the starting left **wing,** skated to the center circle. Because he is the best stickhandler on his team, he takes the opening **face-off.** The referee dropped the puck, and the game was on. From the start, the Coyotes **checked** Paul closely. Everywhere Paul went, a Coyote defenseman followed. The Mighty Duck fans and the national TV audience could see right away that this would be a tight, hard-hitting game.

The Coyotes hoped their tight checking would frustrate Paul. Not a chance. Opponents had put the squeeze on him all season, but because Paul is perhaps the fastest skater in hockey, he's bound to break free. All it takes is a second. A turn of the head. A blink.

Two Coyotes were elbowing Paul along the right boards. Paul had control of the puck. All at once, he whirled and fired a pass through a maze of sticks and skates to teammate J. J. Daigneault at the left circle.

Daigneault flipped it ahead to winger Teemu Selanne, who flicked it into the net for a goal. Roars of joy filled the Arrowhead Pond as the Ducks romped around the ice with glee. Paul's teammates hugged him and he giggled.

Paul had missed the first 11 games of the season with an injury, and the Mighty Ducks won just once without him. "When Paul was out for the first month of the season," coach Ron Wilson said, "it made me truly appreciate what he means to the team." When Paul rejoined the lineup, the Ducks were on their way. They moved up in the standings, then came on in a rush, losing only 3 of their last 23 games. Paul was an easy choice as a finalist for the NHL's Most Valuable Player award.

The Coyotes knew how valuable Paul was, and they clamped down harder on him. So Paul worked harder, too. He got slashed and knocked down but got right back up for more. His silky smooth style and quick bursts of speed were impossible to stop. With four minutes left in the first period, Paul skated through traffic, made a quick change of direction, and was open at the right slot for a shot. With a lightning quick release, he sent the black puck whizzing in a blur toward the goal. It was an atomic blast. The Phoenix goalie had no chance as the blur sliced past his ear into the net. Cheers rang out. White towels twirled in the air. It looked like a blizzard in the

Pond. The Mighty Ducks led 2–0. Magician Paul Kariya had struck again.

The Coyotes scored early in the second period, but the Ducks did not panic. Teemu Selanne, Paul's linemate and roommate on the road, skated the puck in from the **blue line** and rifled a shot off the goalie's leg pad into the net for a 3–1 lead. But the Coyotes scored again on a power play late in the period to make it 3–2. One period remained, and the Ducks had to hang on.

Paul (right) takes a quick break from the action.

The pace was frantic in the final period, as the Coyotes went on the attack. Paul showed his defensive skills by trapping the puck in the **neutral zone** to prevent Phoenix from getting shots at close range. Ducks goalie Guy Hebert made several saves to preserve the lead, and in the dying moments he could barely catch his breath. With a single minute to go, the Coyotes pulled their goalie to add an extra attacker. The substitution was a dangerous move, and Paul made them pay for it. He gained control of the puck and accelerated rapidly as he streaked toward the empty net on a breakaway.

High-scoring forward Teemu Selanne joined the Mighty Ducks in February 1996.

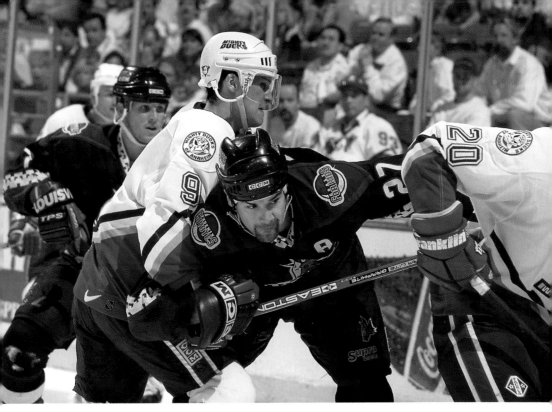

Paul holds his own against the Coyotes.

At the last instant he was tackled by a lunging Coyote. The flagrant foul kept Paul from shooting, and the referee awarded the goal to the Ducks. The fans were on their feet once more, twirling their white towels, and then the horn sounded to end the game. The Mighty Ducks had won 4–2, and Paul was the hero.

Reporters surrounded Paul at his locker and asked him about his great plays. But Paul is a humble superstar. He does not talk about himself. "Hockey is a team game," he told them, "and without my teammates I cannot make plays."

Paul grew up in Vancouver, British Columbia, which lies on
the southern edge of Canada's Pacific coast.

16

2
Learning the Game

Vancouver is a spotless industrial city on an inlet of the Pacific Ocean in the southwest corner of Canada. The city is a wonderful place for a boy to live. The sweet smell of pine needles fills the air in the spring and fall, the white hot sun blisters the sidewalks in summer, and the numbing cold of the wintertime rain refreshes the landscape. Paul was born in Vancouver on October 16, 1974, and he spent the first 14 years of his life here.

Paul's family lived on the north side of town, near English Bay, in a two-story brown house on tree-lined Strathaven Drive. Paul shared a bedroom with his two younger brothers, Steve and Martin. Paul's two younger sisters shared a room down the hall. Paul's mother, Sharon Kariya, was an elementary school teacher until her children's needs grew enough to keep her home.

Paul's full name is Paul Tetsuhiko Kariya, and his middle name is also his father's first name. Tetsuhiko Kariya was born and raised in Canada and is of Japanese heritage. Tetsuhiko works now as a teacher at Argyle Secondary School in Vancouver.

Paul says "I'm very proud of my Japanese heritage," but his loyalty is with his homeland Canada. He has played for Team Canada in national hockey tournaments and the Olympics, just as his father played several tours with the Canadian National Rugby Team. Tetsuhiko played standoff half, which is similar to a quarterback in football, because he was often the best athlete on his team. Paul always wanted to excel at sports like his father.

Paul played all sports as a child. He and his brothers played baseball in the backyard, using a wooden bat and a folded-up sock for the ball. He played roller hockey in the street with the neighborhood kids, and he chipped and putted golf balls outside the house, using soup cans for holes. He played lacrosse, tennis, soccer, and basketball. "At one time I dreamed about playing in the NBA [National Basketball Association]," Paul comments, "I had a pretty good three-point shot."

But Paul's favorite sport was hockey. He began skating at three, and he showed strong ankles and good balance. He practiced figure skating at first, but his parents let him switch to hockey at four.

A SAD FAMILY STORY

During World War II, when Canada and the United States were at war with Japan, Tetsuhiko's parents were shipped along with others of Japanese descent to an internment camp. The Canadian government had felt that so many people of Japanese heritage on the coast could be a threat during this war.

Tetsuhiko's family was moved from a tiny fishing village near Vancouver to the Greenwood Internment Camp in the interior of British Columbia, where they spent six years in captivity. There Tetsuhiko was born and lived the first few years of his life. All possessions had been taken from the Kariya family, and so, Tetsuhiko says, "When we were released, my parents had to start all over again." More than four decades later, Paul's father and grandparents, and thousands of other Canadians, received letters of apology and $21,000 each in restitution from the Canadian government.

"I loved it as soon as I started playing it," he says. At six, he joined his first hockey league in the Tyke Division. "While most kids had a tough time keeping their ankles straight," Tetsuhiko says, "Paul was moving around the ice pretty well."

A year later, Paul moved up to the Novice level and a year after that, to the Atom level, where his father coached Paul's team. While other boys liked to score goals, "Paul liked to set up plays," his father says. "I told him, 'The puck is there, you move it, keep it moving.' That's something we stressed to all our kids—to share." By nine, Paul was playing in the Pee-Wee leagues with kids as old as 14. "There were 6-footers on the ice," says Tetsuhiko, "and Paul was right in there with them."

Behind Paul's house was a woodshed used for storage. Against a side wall stood a stack of cement blocks with fist-sized holes in them. On the ground lay a large piece of slick fiberglass from the wall of a skating rink. Paul and brothers stood on the fiberglass in their tennis shoes and tried to fire a hockey puck through the small holes in the cement blocks. Shots that hit the blocks made a dull thunk sound. Shots through the holes hit the shed with a plink. The boys practiced wrist shots—thunk . . . thunk . . . plink. Slap shots—thunk . . . thunk . . . plink. Big blasts—thunk . . . thunk . . . thunk . . . plink. They practiced all kinds of shots for hours on end. Over time, the side wall of the shed wore down, leaving just strips of plywood covering the holes made by the puck.

Paul "practiced" countless hours inside the house, too. He watched videotapes of great hockey players, the same tapes over and over again, studying the players' habits, memorizing their moves. "I got into visualization early," Paul says. "Where I lived in Vancouver, we didn't get ice time all that much, so I'd watch tapes and think about what I was going to do. I still do that. You watch and think. You learn by osmosis." Paul learned the value of acceleration from tapes of Bobby Orr. He learned the art of passing from watching Mario Lemieux. Mostly though, he learned from Wayne Gretzky, the Great One.

Even as a professional player, Paul watches game videos to help improve his skills.

"Paul enjoys watching a tape of Gretzky from the Canada Cup," said Paul's mother, Sharon. "That's because both are small in stature, and Paul likes to see how Gretzky handles himself in the games. Paul also likes to try some of Gretzky's moves. He also reads quite a bit about Gretzky."

By the age of 11, Paul was skating bent over at the waist, like Gretzky. His movements began to appear effortless, and he liked to set up like Gretzky behind the left side of the net, looking around for teammates. Vancouver Canucks coach Tom Renney saw him play in a junior tournament a year later. "The thing I remember," Renney said, "is that he did things with the puck that other kids his age seemed to have no concept of. He was two and three moves ahead of everyone else. Even then, he was a very creative, imaginative, and intuitive player."

Paul was an Edmonton Oilers fan because Gretzky played for that team. Paul's mother had to console her son when the Oilers traded Gretzky in 1988 to the Los Angeles Kings. Little did Paul know that he, too, would someday be playing NHL hockey in southern California. For the time being, he remained loyal to Gretzky, watching his idol skate for the Kings and studying old tapes. "I watch Gretzky in my spare time because we're about the same size," Paul said. "The way he uses his teammates and finds open people. The game seems to slow down when he has the puck.

Since he joined the Mighty Ducks, Paul has had the opportunity to play against hockey legend Wayne Gretzky, Paul's childhood idol.

He does things with style, with class. I want to do things in a similar way. I've just tried to take the best things I've seen of Gretzky from the tapes."

Paul studied hard in school too. His parents were schoolteachers and they insisted that their children read books and study. Paul attended Argyle Secondary School, where his father taught math and computer science. He got mostly A's. "School was very important in our household," Paul says. "We didn't watch much TV because we were doing homework or playing sports." But schoolwork came first, and sports second, as Paul found out one day.

The Argyle rugby team was scheduled to play rival Handsworth School in the North Shore Bantam League championship game. Paul starred for Argyle as the scrum half, the link between forwards and backs, and his father was the team's coach. The players had to leave school early the day of the championship game to be bussed to Handsworth. Paul had told his father several days earlier that he had a test that afternoon. "Make sure you arrange for a make-up test with your teacher," Paul's father told him. But Paul forgot.

The day of the game, the team assembled in the school parking lot and Paul told his father his predicament. "You didn't reschedule your test?" his father said. "Go take your test." The team filed onto the bus, Paul's father climbed aboard, and the bus drove off without Paul. After Paul took his test, a PE teacher drove him to Handsworth, and Paul played in the second half. Argyle won 3–0.

Paul got along well with his friends at Argyle. He also maintained a 3.8 grade-point average, even getting an A in his father's 9th-grade math class. But life was soon about to change. At 15, his hockey skills were so polished that he had trouble finding competition his age. His parents realized that Paul's dream of playing pro hockey was within reach. They arranged for Paul to go away to Penticton, a small community about 200 miles east of Vancouver. There he would enter a year-round hockey program and also attend school.

3
Leaving Home

The British Columbia Junior Hockey League was forming a new team, the Penticton Panthers. Penticton was a hockey hotbed, with several strong junior league teams, and other future NHL players—like Andy Moog, Joe Murphy, and Brett Hull—had gone through the program there. Penticton also had a fine school, and that's what Paul's parents liked best. Paul moved there in the summer of 1990.

Garry Davidson was the Penticton coach. Before the program in Penticton began, Davidson had been coaching hockey in Italy. Even as far away as Europe, though, Davidson had heard about a speedy young skater playing on Canada's west coast—Paul Kariya. "When I returned to Canada to start the Panthers, I went to Vancouver to recruit Paul, even though I'd never seen him play," says Davidson. "He was even better than I'd heard." Davidson saw Paul play at an evaluation camp of the top 46 junior players of western British Columbia. "He was the best player there," Davidson said. "He was very creative, and he made some passes I couldn't believe anyone could make."

Paul moved in with the Stork family on Cambie Street. Roberta and Jerry Stork had taken in junior hockey players before, and their son Dean always looked forward to meeting his new housemate. Paul got his own room on the bottom level of the two-story house, and the first thing he did was put up his three posters of Wayne Gretzky.

Paul poses with his mother, Sharon (upper left) and Jerry and Roberta Stork (lower left and right).

Paul became good friends with Dean Stork (left), who later went to the University of Massachusetts on a hockey scholarship.

Paul and Dean became fast friends. They played darts and shot pool, went swimming and golfing, and smacked hockey pucks around the yard so much they left hundreds of black skid marks everywhere. "He was so different from the other hockey players we had stay with us," Roberta says. "He was competitive and fun, but he was very polite and serious, too. He was so mature."

At tryouts for the Panthers, 170 boys showed up. Paul was the youngest of the bunch. Most of the boys were 17 or 18. Some were as old as 20, the league age limit. Paul was 15. But age doesn't always matter in hockey. Paul was the best player. Not only did he make the team, but coach Davidson named him captain.

Paul played at center the first game, and then he switched to **wing,** which allowed him to stretch the defense with his speed. The Panthers won three of their four exhibition games, and folks in Penticton took notice. "He's a super player," coach Davidson said about Paul. "He's the most talented player I've ever dealt with. His skill level—his handling of the puck, his ability to pass, his ability to read and react—is exceptional. Sure he imitates Gretzky, but I'm not about to say anything to Paul about that."

The regular season was a nightmare. The Panthers had few skilled players other than Paul, which allowed teams to gang up on him. Weighing just 130 pounds, Paul was far smaller than his opponents, but he was so quick and intelligent he could escape harm most times. Most times. He took his share of checks and punches. One time he got smacked by a stick so hard in the face that it left a snatch of splinters in his cheek and knocked out four teeth. He spent the next several hours undergoing major dental surgery. With opponents smothering Paul, the Panthers won just 13 of 60 games. Yet Paul was elusive enough to score 45 goals and assist on 67 more, and he was honored as the British Columbia Junior Hockey League Player of the Year. He was the youngest winner ever.

Paul was a success in school, too. He paid close attention in class, studied hard, and impressed the teachers. "He always had his books with him," senior counselor Bob Syer remembers. "He was all about business. Hockey was hockey, but when he was here at school, Paul was here to learn."

One book Paul always kept with him was an autobiography of Wayne Gretzky. Computer teacher Gord Barnes liked to play a game with Paul. Barnes would search through the book for the smallest details he could find and make up a list of 10 questions. Barnes was a Vancouver Canucks fan, and if he could stump Paul on a question, Paul would have to wear the teacher's Canucks jersey at school for a day. "I never could stump him," says Barnes. "He always got every question right. He never wore that Canucks jersey."

Paul's senior year arrived and he sensed the importance of it. He knew he would play college hockey, but he wanted his choice of schools. College recruiters had shown up at Penticton's games, but most times they watched Paul's team lose. How good could a player be if his team always lost? Paul took no chances. Everything he did from then on, every decision he made, every step he took, was connected in some way to hockey.

Paul's new game at the Storks' house was to tap a golf ball or tennis ball around the carpet without looking. He would hold his head up and run around the pool table or through the living room batting the ball. The Storks would tease him about being so serious and he would say, "It's not talent that makes a good hockey player, it's hard work." He would eat only pastas, fruits and salads, and a bit of protein. His only treat was a single bowl of cereal each night before bed. "You have to set a goal and focus," he would say. "Set a goal and focus."

Paul was a star on the ice. His artful skating and crisp passes were nearly impossible to stop, and the Panthers began to win more games than they lost. In an early-season game at Merritt, an all-league defenseman followed him around the ice, elbowing him and jabbing at him with his stick. Paul played through it, made two goals and four assists, and Penticton won 7-6. "That was a special night for Paul," said coach Davidson. "He learned that night how to deal with very close checking."

The attention on Paul grew overwhelming. Crowds of college recruiters pressed against the boards at games to watch him. Minor league scouts constantly called him at home and at school. He was a blue-chip prospect, among the most heavily recruited seniors in all of North America. His privacy was gone and sometimes it was nearly too much to bear.

Paul was in class one day when he got another phone call. A recruiter again? A scout? No, it was coach Davidson. Paul went to the office and put the phone to his ear. All of a sudden he started jumping up and down and screaming, "I made the team! I made the team!" Coach Davidson told Paul that he had been selected to play for the Team Canada Juniors in the World Games. "It was the only time I ever saw Paul act like a little kid," Gord Barnes remembers. "He came running out of the office yelling, 'I get to play with Eric Lindros!' I never saw him so excited."

Paul missed seven games with the Panthers to play for Team Canada. He joined Eric Lindros and the rest of the Junior Team in Germany, where they played six games against international competition.

Paul relaxes with Brian Barnes, a friend who also played on the Penticton Panthers hockey team.

Paul and Eric Lindros met up frequently over the years, this time at an NHL awards ceremony in 1996.

Paul and Eric became friends, sharing stories about sticks and skates and camps. Paul managed to skate well enough to get a goal and an assist. But by the end of the trip, he was worn out. On the flight home, Eric advised Paul to get some rest. "You should take at least a week off," Eric said. "You have to give yourself a break." But Paul didn't listen.

Upon returning to Penticton, Paul re-packed his suitcase and left again. He went with coach Davidson and Panthers owner Mark Wagstaff to Victoria where he was picked to play in the British Columbia Junior All-Star Game. Paul felt exhausted during the five-hour ride to Victoria.

As he stood in the lobby of the Ingraham Hotel to check in, Paul began to feel dizzy. All at once he collapsed. Coach Davidson and Mark Wagstaff and other people nearby frantically revived him and lifted him to his feet. They helped him into the elevator and up to his room where they put him in bed. A doctor ordered him to stay there for 48 hours.

He missed the all-star game, of course. Back in Penticton two days later, doctors told Paul he had an infection called mononucleosis. He missed Penticton's next 12 games.

"I made a mistake," Paul admitted. "Eric Lindros told me I should take off at least a week after the World Games, but I didn't. And because I got so run down, a flu bug became mono."

Paul rested and did his schoolwork at home, and when he returned to the ice, it was as if he had never left. University of Maine assistant coach Grant Standbrook was among the recruiters to see Paul the night he returned. Coach Standbrook had already seen Paul play, but he was sitting with Larry Ross, a scout for the San Jose Sharks, who hadn't. "I told Larry not to expect too much," coach Standbrook said, "because Paul was just getting off an illness." What did Paul do? He scored four goals and made an assist in his team's 5–4 win.

Paul finished the year with 46 goals and 86 assists in just 40 games. He broke all of Brett Hull's Penticton scoring records. The Panthers won 37 games to finish second in the 10-team league, and Paul was chosen as the Junior Player of the Year for all of Canada. "The thing that sets him apart from everyone else is that he's got Larry Bird court sense," said Jack Parker of Boston University, one of many coaches trying to sign Paul. "He sees everyone and he knows when to deliver the puck and when to hold on."

Paul always seemed to make the right decision with the puck. Now he had to decide about college. He had been accepted to every hockey powerhouse across North America. What would be his choice? Or would he even choose college? He had been offered $200,000 to sign with the Tri-Cities Americans of Western Hockey League. His parents could use that money. Paul gave the decision some thought. Then he visited school counselor Dave Lee.

"I'm not going to tell you what to do," counselor Lee said in his office. "But I think education is the right way to go."

"Yes," Paul agreed, "but that's an awful lot of money."

"Fine. But what if you get injured? Or what if the club folds? Then there's no money. And no education."

"Well," Paul said before leaving, "I want to think about it some more."

"Fine, Paul. You think about it. Take your time."

Paul thought for another week before making his decision. He chose college. "Paul's mother desperately wanted me to convince Paul to go to college," Lee remembers. "I couldn't convince Paul of anything because he was mature enough to make up his own mind. But his mother sure was thrilled with his choice."

Paul was excited, too. He chose the University of Maine-Orono, because the town of Orono, Maine, reminded him of Penticton, "only colder." And he said choosing education over money was easy once he thought about it. "I've always thought college hockey," he said, "was a great place to learn the game."

Paul announces his decision to attend the University of Maine.

4

The Maine Man

A record crowd of 5,442 crammed into Alfond Arena for the University of Maine's 1992 season opener against Providence College. Paul was so excited the night before that he hardly slept. But he was also nervous. The Hockey East League had a tough reputation, and he wasn't sure what to expect.

Paul had seen Maine's arena filled like this two weeks earlier, when the team was divided in half to play in the traditional Blue-White scrimmage. Five thousand people for a practice! That's how fanatical Maine hockey fans are. This was a special year for the Black Bears though, and the whole state was buzzing. Maine had been ranked No. 1 in a national poll. Although the Black Bears hadn't played any games yet, they looked good on paper. The team boasted a front line of senior Jim Montgomery, wily Cal Ingraham, and a new kid—a phenom by the name of Paul

Kariya. They also had the Ferraro twins, Chris and Peter, and goalies Mike Dunham and Garth Snow.

The team looked good on the ice, too. They blistered Providence with nine goals. Paul got his first, along with two assists. Jim Montgomery had wondered just how good Paul would be, and he got his answer on their first line shift together. "I was wide open a couple of times and I started yelling his name," Montgomery says. "We get back to the bench and he says to me, 'Jim, I don't like it when you yell out there. You don't have to yell. I know you're there.' Right then I thought, 'God, this guy is going to be great.'"

The Black Bears went to Fairbanks, Alaska, where they swept three games at the Great Alaska Face-Off Tournament. Maine coach Shawn Walsh discovered how bright Paul was at this tournament. The morning of the first game, Paul approached Walsh with a question. "Coach," he said, "which bench will we have tonight?"

Coach Walsh wondered what Paul was getting at. "Why?" he asked.

"Because," Paul said, "I like to visualize which goal I'll be skating toward."

Coach Walsh knew right then he had a special player. "This guy's mind," Walsh realized, "is at a higher level." Paul's visualization technique worked at the tournament. He had three goals and three assists and was named MVP.

Paul and teammate Jim Montgomery celebrate a win.

Back at Maine, Paul studied hard and made the dean's list, which is like making the all-league team in academics. He worked hard at hockey too, staying on the practice ice long after others had left it, refining his skills and rehearsing new tricks. He was a perfectionist with his sticks, leaning over them day after day, filing them like a craftsman. A perfectly curved blade meant a perfect pass or a perfect shot.

The Black Bears were 11–0–1 in early December, when they were nearly upset by Northeastern. After narrowly winning 5–4 and going home to think about their near-loss, they returned to Alfond Arena the following night to play the Huskies again. Paul wouldn't let them come close to losing this time. He scored a goal and had a school-record five assists in an 11–2 raking. "All you have to do is get your stick free, and Paul will get you the puck," Montgomery told reporters in the team's locker room. "You don't have to be open, just your stick." Paul heard Jim's words and blushed. When the reporters asked Paul about his artful setups he said, "When I was growing up, I played with older players. And they all wanted to score. So I had no choice but to pass. Even now, in my brain, I'm saying pass first, shoot second. Sometimes that gets me in trouble. But I like to think that 99 percent of the time the pass is the right play."

Paul took time out midway through the year to play again for the Team Canada Juniors in the World Games. This time Paul went to bed early and got plenty of rest. During seven games in Sweden, he scored two goals and six assists to lead Team Canada to the gold. Paul returned to Maine to a hero's welcome and was happy to learn his team had won all six games while he was away.

With Paul back, the Black Bears kept on winning. They ran their mark to 30–0–2 as Paul set Hockey East freshman records for points and assists. "We don't want to lose a game," he said. The Black Bears lost their very next game. It was a heart-wrenching defeat at home to rival Boston University. Boston won

7–6 in overtime, after the Bears had led 6–2. The loss was painful, and the Bears vowed not to let it happen again. First they avenged the defeat by beating Boston University 5–2 in the Hockey East title game. Then they steamrolled through the National Collegiate Athletic Association playoffs over powerhouses Minnesota and Michigan to reach the NCAA championship game.

Paul had set Maine scoring records with 75 assists and 100 points, and he had been an easy choice for Hockey East Player of the Year. The night before the college title game at the Bradley Center in Milwaukee, Wisconsin, Paul learned he had won another award. He received the Hobey Baker Award, presented to the nation's premier college hockey player.

Paul holds up the trophy he received for winning the Hobey Baker Award in 1993.

He was the first freshman ever to win it. Paul was shocked and embarrassed. He thanked his teammates and coaches and everyone he could think of. But he declined to talk about himself. "This is a team award," he said. "It is a tremendous honor, but you can't win something like this without the help and support of your teammates."

The following night in front of a record crowd of 17,704 in Milwaukee, Paul showed why he was college hockey's best player. Maine trailed Lake Superior State 4–2 with one period to go. The Lakers were defending NCAA champions and a tough-minded defensive bunch. Inside the Maine locker room, assistant coach Red Gendron told Paul, "Keep your feet moving along the boards and you'll beat your guy." Paul listened.

Scoring three goals in one period would not be easy. Paul found a way early on in the game. Fending off two opponents, Paul stole the puck behind the Lakers net, skated in front, and slid the puck across the goal mouth to Montgomery, who rammed it in. "I kept my feet moving," Paul said. Three minutes later he started a play out of his **zone** and across **center ice** where he lifted a pass over a defender's stick to Chris Imes, who poked it ahead to Montgomery, who shot it in off a Laker defenseman. The Black Bears had tied it 4–4. Midway through the period, Paul skated across the blue line around a defender and waited for someone to get open. Montgomery did. Paul brushed a perfect pass, soft and along the ice, to the right post. Montgomery tapped it in. Maine led 5–4. The Black Bears stifled the Lakers in the final minutes to win the championship, and Paul was suddenly part of a wild celebration at center ice.

"My linemates aren't just my linemates, they're my best friends," Paul said afterward. "So the fact that we came back and did it together is just amazing. If I never play another hockey game, this would be a nice way to end my career."

Others would not let that happen. Owners and coaches of the National Hockey League were drooling at the idea of getting Paul on their team. He was still just 18, but the NHL draft was coming up, and somebody was going to draft him early, because he was too good to pass up. The Winter Olympics would be staged at the end of the year, and Team Canada wanted him too. And then there was college. "I'm open to everything," Paul said. "I really enjoy Maine and I'd love to come back. But playing for the Canadian Olympic team would be a great opportunity and playing in the NHL would also be great."

The NHL draft was held at the Le Colisee in Quebec City, and Paul was there. The Anaheim Mighty Ducks hoped Paul would be available when they picked fourth. Anaheim General Manager Jack Ferreira and assistant Pierre Gauthier had seen Paul in the NCAA tournament. In the second period of the semifinal game, Ferreira had turned to Gauthier and whispered, "This guy's a home run." Paul had no idea Anaheim was interested in him. Most teams spoke with him several times in the days leading up to the draft to learn more about him. But Anaheim's plan was to avoid being seen anywhere near Paul. The Ducks knew whom they wanted, and they didn't want to tip anyone off.

Alexandre Daigle was chosen first, by Ottawa. The San Jose Sharks, who drafted second, were rumored to be interested in Paul, but they traded their pick to Hartford, who used it for defenseman Chris Pronger. The hearts of Mighty Ducks officials were dancing now, and owner Michael Eisner couldn't help glancing Paul's way. Maine coach Shawn Walsh, who was sitting with Paul, realized something was up when Eisner winked at him. The Tampa Bay Devil Rays picked third. They announced center Chris Gratton as their choice, and the Ducks nearly jumped out of their seats. At 12:47 pm, 42 minutes after the draft began, Anaheim called out the name Paul Kariya.

The Mighty Ducks knew Paul's other dream was to play in the Olympics. The NHL season would start in October and the Olympics would take place two months later in the heart of the season. Paul couldn't do both. The Ducks told him he could skip the season. He could join the team the following year.

Paul led the Black Bears to win the 1993 NCAA
Championship. His NHL deal with the Mighty Ducks would
allow him to play a few more games with the Black Bears in
the 1993–1994 season.

Paul played the first 12 games for Maine, racking up 8 goals and 16 assists. Then he said goodbye to his college friends and joined Team Canada. "He is by far the most creative player in college hockey, maybe in its history," coach Walsh said. "He'll be an offensive catalyst for Canada." Paul was the youngest player on the Canadian team. Yet he was named the center for the first line. His wingers were NHL veterans Chris Contos and Petr Nedved. Paul fit right in. In 31 games on a two-month pre-Olympic tour, he had 10 goals and 38 assists.

The 1994 Olympic Games were held in Lillehammer, Norway. Paul was just one of 1,884 athletes from 67 countries, but he stood as proudly as anyone. In Canada's first game, he sparked his team to a 7–2 victory over Italy with three assists. The Canadians sailed through five games of pool play with one loss. Then they beat the Czech Republic in the quarterfinals when Paul scored a dramatic goal in overtime.

Team Canada hadn't won the Olympic hockey gold since 1952, but it moved within a step by defeating Finland in the semifinals. The gold medal game at Hakon Hall was the final event of the 16-day sports festival. The closing ceremony would be staged an hour after it ended. But Canada and Sweden battled fiercely in a game that seemed to never end.

Sweden took a 1–0 lead in the first period and held it until midway through the third, when Paul slapped a rebound past the goalie to tie the score. Two minutes later, Canada took the lead on Derek Mayer's wrist shot. But with 1 minute 49 seconds left in the game and the Canadians on the verge of triumph, Sweden's Magnus Svensson scored on a slap shot. The game went to sudden death. After a frantic 10-minute overtime, the score was still tied. After a shootout, in which each team had five different players slam the puck at the goalie, the game remained deadlocked. Paul had scored one of his team's two goals in the shootout, but Sweden also had scored twice. Finally they entered a sudden-death shootout, in which one goal would decide the winner. Sweden shot first and missed. Canada's Petr Nedved went next with a chance to win the gold. He missed too. Sweden's Peter Forsberg went next. He flew in, faked right, went left, and wristed the puck beneath Canadian goalie Corey Hirsch's glove. It was up to Paul. A goal would force another tie. A miss and it would be over. Paul skated in on Swedish goalie Tommy Salo and smoked a forehand shot. Salo kicked it away with his left leg. Team Sweden won. The Canadians would have to settle for the silver. The Swedes piled on top of Forsberg. Paul stood motionless. He peeked at the celebration, but mostly he looked down at the ice.

Paul had grown used to winning. But he would have to handle defeat too. He was about to join the Mighty Ducks.

5

A Mighty Star

Anaheim Mighty Ducks general manager Jack Ferreira and coach Ron Wilson showed up one day at Paul's house on Strathaven Drive to offer him a contract. They ate dinner with Paul's family and discussed a multi-year deal for millions of dollars. When they were finished eating, Paul's mother turned to him.

"Paul," she said, "clear the dishes."

Paul rose quietly and got to work. "He didn't bat an eye," Wilson remembers. "Away he went, no harrumphs, nothing."

After Paul washed the dishes, everyone went to the living room to talk more. "We brought along all the Anaheim Ducks shirts and hats and stuff we could find, and we put them on a couch," Wilson says. "The younger kids were looking at it all, but no one made a move. The pile just sat there until after dinner when the parents said it was all right to inspect the things we brought." Paul ended up signing a three-year deal with the Ducks for $6.4 million. But he still had to do the dishes.

Paul moved to Orange County, California, in the fall. Rather than buy a fancy bachelor pad though, he rented a room in a house owned by Gary and Teri Frederick. "He goes to bed at 9:30, maybe 10 o'-clock," Teri said. "The rest of us are still sitting up, watching television. He doesn't even want his own telephone. I suggested it, thought he'd want to make some calls, but he said he didn't need a telephone. He thought it would be a bother."

Paul wanted to concentrate on hockey with the Ducks. But he would have to wait. The owners and players had been arguing all summer over money and they didn't settle in time to start the season. With the season on hold, Paul added six pounds of muscle by weight training. He also learned to juggle. "I had a book, *Lessons from the Art of Juggling*," he said. "It's really about more than learning how to juggle. Juggling is a metaphor for life. I followed the lessons, though. I can do the one where you take the bite out of the apple as it comes by. If it gives you just that split second more of coordination, it's something you have."

The hockey dispute eventually was settled, and the Mighty Ducks opened the season in Edmonton.

Paul juggles hockey pucks for fun.

The Northlands Coliseum had long been the home of Paul's hero Wayne Gretzky, and Paul got goosebumps just thinking about it. Even though the Ducks lost 2–1, Paul still considers that game his favorite moment in the pros. "He's everything his press clippings said he was," Edmonton coach Glen Sather said afterward. "He's intelligent, aggressive, a very dedicated skater. He's going to be one of the new stars of the NHL."

One night later, Paul scored his first Ducks goal in a 4–3 win at Winnipeg. But Paul found that the NHL game moved much faster than college hockey. He would have to react more quickly to dodge his opponents, and it took Paul some time to adjust. He got bumped and checked and hurt, and when the team returned to Edmonton in February, Paul had to sit out with a sore back. That was the only game he missed all season. In mid-March, he went on an eight-game scoring streak, and he finished the season as the team leader in most scoring categories. But the Ducks finished with a 16–27–5 record and placed sixth in the Pacific Division.

Paul scored more goals than any other NHL rookie, and he was the only rookie to lead his team in scoring. Paul wasn't comfortable with shooting so much, but the Ducks were a defense-minded team with no firepower other than him. So coach Wilson told him to plan to shoot more. He would have to be the team's scoring threat for now. Paul spent the off-season lifting heavy weights, adding more muscle to his body. He amazed his teammates with his three-hour workouts. "Getting better every day," Paul said. "That's what this game is all about."

Paul's team opened the 1995–96 season with a goal in Winnipeg. His wicked slap shot from the top of the circle echoed through the arena. Two nights later, he scored twice more. "Wow," coach Wilson said. "He's a natural."

Paul had always been the playmaker, and he was beginning to enjoy this new role as a scorer. He shot the game-winning goal two nights later in Buffalo, scored the team's lone goal in its home opener against Vancouver, and scored twice more in a home win over Calgary. His wrist shot was often too fast for the goalie to react. "It's so quick, it's scary," Wilson said.

"I'd always been told growing up that I had a good shot," Paul said. "I had good technique and everything. I just never used it. I didn't have the strength. Now I'm stronger, my release is better, and the more I shoot, the more confidence I get."

Paul was named to the NHL All-Star team as a starting left wing. During introductions he stood next to Teemu Selanne, another young speedster who played for Winnipeg, and together they stared in awe. "Every time a player was introduced," Selanne recalls, "we'd say, 'What a player he is' . . . 'He's a great player' . . . 'He's unbelievable too.'" Paul had a goal and an assist in the game, and he impressed the other stars. "With his speed and quickness and tenacity," Blues sharpshooter Brett Hull said, "he's a true superstar."

Three weeks later Paul heard some wonderful news. The Ducks had just acquired Teemu Selanne in a trade. Paul knew the ice would open up for him now. "This will change the way I play the game," he said.With the league's two fastest wingers skating together, Anaheim made a rush for the playoffs. "I've played with a lot of great players, guys like Eric Lindros, and we've had good chemistry," Paul said, "but not the kind of chemistry Teemu and I have. It's so much fun playing the game when you know exactly what the other person's going to do." The Mighty Ducks won six straight games in March and lost just one of their last eight to finish the season. But they had started the season so poorly, they still missed the playoffs in a tiebreaker.

Paul's 50 goals and 58 assists ranked among the league leaders, and his four penalty minutes were an

NHL low. "I don't go out thinking I want to be the cleanest player in the league," he said. "but if I'm playing the game properly, I should never get a penalty." Paul was awarded the Lady Byng Trophy, which honors the player who best combines sportsmanship and playing excellence. "It's a great feeling," Paul said. "I'm really thankful for it."

Paul's excellent puck-handling skills stand out even among the best and most experienced NHL players.

What Paul wanted above anything was a trip to the playoffs. And that's just what he got in 1997. He missed the first 11 games of the 1996–97 season with an abdominal strain, and the Mighty Ducks won just once without him. He returned to energize the team and Ducks moved up steadily in the standings. Paul had been named team captain at the start of the season, and though he didn't speak much, he didn't have to. After a midday practice, defenseman David Karpa cranked up the volume on the locker-room stereo. Paul gave him a glare. No words. Just a glare. "Oh, excuse me, excuse me," Karpa said, "we can't do this while Paul is having one of his conferences." Karpa quickly turned down the stereo.

Paul had a five-point game against Calgary, scored a hat trick against Buffalo, set the club record for fastest goal eight seconds into the game at Colorado, scored a goal again at the All-Star game, and skated his team into the 1997 playoffs. In the seven-game quarterfinal series against the Phoenix Coyotes, Paul's team won the first two games at home, but then lost the next three. Facing elimination at America West Arena in Phoenix, the Mighty Ducks won 3–2 in overtime when Paul fired a wrist shot from a tough angle past the Phoenix goalie. "An unbelievable shot," linemate Steve Rucchin said. The Ducks thumped Phoenix 3–0 in the deciding game to advance.

The team's hopes were scuttled in the semifinal

series however, as the eventual Stanley Cup champion Detroit Red Wings swept them in four games. Still it was a rewarding year, as Paul was named one of three finalists for Hart Memorial Trophy, honoring the league MVP. He had 44 goals and 55 assists to finish third in scoring, though he probably doesn't know it. He doesn't keep track of such things. He doesn't read hockey reports in the newspaper. He only knows his goal total because it's announced after each one. "You don't accomplish anything by looking backwards," he says. "Life isn't lived backwards."

Playing for the Disney-owned Mighty Ducks, Paul gets all the free passes he wants to Disneyland, as well as free tickets to Disney movies. He is aware of his good fortune and he understands the responsibility that comes with it. "I think people see anyone who is in the public eye as a role model to some degree," he says. "I realize I'm one of those people and have a responsibility to the fans and to the Ducks organization to be a good person and a good citizen, as well as a good hockey player."

But Paul didn't become a good person because he had to. He was a good person before he ever became a superstar hockey player, or a millionaire, or even an expert juggler. "What my parents taught me," he says, "is that it doesn't matter what you do in life, whether you're a businessman or a garbageman, you've got to be a good person."

Career Highlights

Regular Season Statistics

Minor Leagues	Team	Games	Goals	Assists	Points
1990–91	Penticton (BCJHL)	54	45	67	112
1991–92	Penticton (BCJHL)	40	46	86	132
1992–93	U. of Maine (NCAA)	39	25	75	100
1993–94	Canada (Intn'l)	31	10	38	48
1993–94	U. of Maine (NCAA)	12	8	16	24
Totals		176	134	282	416
NHL					
1994–95	Anaheim	47	18	21	39
1995–96	Anaheim	82	50	58	108
1996–97	Anaheim	69	44	55	99
Totals		198	112	134	246

NHL Playoff Statistics

Season	Team	Games	Goals	Assists	Points
1994–95	Anaheim	—	—	—	—
1995–96	Anaheim	—	—	—	—
1996–97	Anaheim	11	7	6	13
Totals		11	7	6	13

Honors
- Won Hobey Baker Memorial Award in 1993
- Won Lady Byng Memorial Trophy in 1996
- Named Hockey East Player of the Year in 1993
- Named Hockey East Rookie of the Year in 1993
- Named to NCAA All-America East first team in 1993
- Named to NCAA All-Tournament team in 1993
- Named to Hockey East All-Star first team in 1993
- Named to Hockey East All-Rookie team in 1993
- Named to Hockey East All-Decade team in 1994
- Named to NHL All-Rookie team in 1995
- Named to NHL All-Star first team in 1996
- Played in NHL All-Star Game in 1996 and 1997

Glossary

blue line: One of two 1-foot-wide blue lines that indicate where a team's offensive zone (and the other team's defensive zone) begins. The blue line is 60 feet from the goal line.

center ice: The neutral zone between the two blue lines.

check: The use of one's body or stick to take the puck away from an opponent or to block or hit the opponent so that that player loses control of the puck.

face-off: The act of dropping the puck between two opposing players to start or resume play. A face-off is held to start each period, after every goal, and after every stoppage of play.

neutral zone: The area of ice between the blue lines.

power play: The offense used when one's team has more players on the ice because the other team has one or more players in the penalty box.

shorthanded: A team with fewer players on the ice than its opponent is said to be playing shorthanded.

wing: A forward who plays on the left or right side.

wrist shot: A shot in which the shooter keeps his or her stick on the ice and generates the power for the shot by snapping his or her wrists.

zone: A team's zone, or defending zone, is the area between that team's goal and the nearest blue line.

Sources

Information for this book was obtained from the following sources: Interviews with Gord Barnes, Garry Davidson, Tetsuhiko Kariya, Dave Lee, Roberta Stork, Bob Syer. Kevin Allen (*USA TODAY*, 12 November 1992); Steve Bisheff (*Orange County Register*, 4 December 1996); Earl Bloom (*Orange County Register*, 27 June 1993); Cammy Clark (*St. Petersburg Times*, 6 December 1995); Jim Concannon (*Boston Globe*, 4 April 1993); Karen Crouse (*Orange County Register*, 20 June 1996); Karen Crouse (*Fort Lauderdale Sun-Sentinel*, 1 January 1997); Steve Dryden (*The Hockey News Yearbook*, 1996-1997); Danny Evans (*Orange Coast*, November 1995); Jim Greenidge (*Boston Globe*, 1 November 1992); Mike Guersch (*San Jose Mercury News*, 16 January 1997); Michael Knisley (*The Sporting News*, 14 February 1994); Mike Lowe (*Maine Sunday Telegram*, 28 February 1993); Roy MacGregor (*Ottawa Citizen*, 30 April 1996); Michael Madden (*Boston Globe*, 4 April 1993); Larry Mahoney (*Bangor Daily News*, 3 April 1993, 24 June 1993); Leigh Montville (*Sports Illustrated*, 13 February 1995); Austin Murphy (*Sports Illustrated*, 28 April 1997); Robyn Norwood (*Los Angeles Times*, 27 November 1995, 6 April 1996, 28 December 1996); Mike Penner (*Los Angeles Times*, 27 June 1993); Matt Sullivan (*College Sports*, December 1993); and E.M. Swift (*Sports Illustrated*, 22 February 1993).

Index

Write to Paul:

You can send mail to Paul at the address on the right. If you write a letter, don't get your hopes up too high. Paul and other athletes get lots of letters every day, and they aren't always able to answer them all.

Mr. Paul Kariya
c/o Anaheim Mighty Ducks
Arrowhead Pond of Anaheim
2695 Katella Avenue
Anaheim, CA 92806

Acknowledgments

Photographs are reproduced with the permission of: pp. 1, 57, Sports-Chrome East/West; pp. 2, 6, © ALLSPORT USA/Glenn Cratty; p. 9, © ALLSPORT USA/Stephen Dunn; pp. 10, 13, 15, 21, 53, © V. J. Lovero; p. 14, SportsChrome East/West, Scott Brinegar; p. 16, Duncan McDougall/Diarama Stock Photos; p. 19, National Archives of Canada, #C46350; p. 23, © Debora Robinson; p. 26, © Danny's Photography/Roberta and Jerry Stork; pp. 28, 29, 33; Roberta and Jerry Stork; p. 34, © ALLSPORT USA/Rick Stewart; pp. 25, 37, 38, 41, 47, © Monty Rand Photography; pp. 43, 50, 54, AP/Wide World Photos.

Front cover photograph by SportsChrome East/West and back cover photograph © ALLSPORT USA/Sylvia Pecota.

Artwork by Sean Todd.

About the Author

Jeff Savage was born in Oakland, California, and grew up in nearby Fremont. He graduated from the University of California at San Diego in 1988 with a degree in journalism and worked as a sportswriter for eight years at the San Diego Union-Tribune. He is the author of more than 30 books for young readers. In addition to his work as a writer, Jeff plays golf, practices karate, and flies airplanes. He lives with his wife, Nancy, and son, Taylor, in Napa, California.